The Common Loon

Written by Terry L. Miller
Designed by Bob Lynch

Copyright © 1987 by
THE CARTWHEEL CO.
318 Chester Street St. Paul, Minnesota 55107

ISBN 0-934520-26-7

PRINTED IN HONG KONG
FOR TERRELL PUBLISHING CO.

TABLE OF CONTENTS

INTRODUCTION

ON A COOL SUMMER EVENING in the upper regions of North America, a wailing call resounds across the lakes. Its enchantment echos through the souls of all creatures present and emanates from a feathered symbol of all that is wild – the Common Loon. For many it is a reminder that man has not tamed all things.

In North America a fascination with the Common Loon has steadily grown in recent years. Its call, beauty, and visibility on breeding grounds of the northern United States and Canada are factors contributing to this excitement.

In times past certain native Americans have held the Loon in great honor, while others used it as a source of food. In either case, Loons and man lived in harmony. The early white settler did not entertain such a belief concerning our wildlife and our land. He existed to pursue and conquer, reassuring himself that he was dominant. Now, as wild things have become rare, he has tried to correct his past mistakes and limit his present ones.

Caught up in this renewed dedication to our environment, the Common Loon has won the hearts of many people, much more so than our other three species of Loons. Perhaps it is because the Arctic, Red-throated, and Yellow-billed Loons occupy ranges much farther north. While all four species will be described, the life history of the Common Loon shall be our focal point. It is our hope, with these descriptions and spectacular photography, to provide insight into the life of the Common Loon. — *Terry L. Miller*

EVOLUTIONARY HISTORY

The Common Loon (*Gavia immer*) is a species that has survived longer than any other flying bird species presently living on earth. For approximately 60 million years the Common Loon has adapted to various flora and fauna as fluctuating climates changed its environment. Adapting to changing climates has been a small achievement compared to the ongoing struggle it has survived with man. Man has had a more dramatic effect on the ecological balance of the world than any other species, though the problems man has created are geologically very young. His effect on the environment and on Loons will be covered later in greater detail.

Loons represent one of the most primitive groups of birds alive in the world today. Their anatomy and fossil record has been studied, along with most organisms known to man, and has resulted in a system of evolutionary classification. The Loons' phylogeny or taxonomic classification that depicts their evolutionary history is as follows:

Kingdom Animalia
Phylum Chordata
Sub-Phylum Vertebrata
Class Aves (Birds)
Order Gaviiformes
Family Gaviidae
Genus *Gavia*

Only four species of this single family are known. They are the Common Loon (*Gavia immer*), Yellow-billed Loon (*Gavia adamsii*),

Red-throated Loon (*Gavia stellata*), and the Arctic Loon (*Gavia artica*). Although the Grebes (Order Podicipediformes) possess similarities with Loons, a direct evolutionary relationship is not thought to exist. Now, before we examine Loons in detail, let us look at the history of birds as a whole.

All birds are believed to have been descendants of reptiles. A 140 million-year-old fossil called *Archaeopteryx* possessed characteristics of both birds and reptiles. It had scales on its legs and head along with a feathered body. The bill possessed teeth and the bend of the wings held claws. Flight was probably desired by reptiles to capture flying insects which had already dominated the air. *Archaeopteryx* may have been an advanced form of tree-dwelling reptiles that slowly modified their scales to trap heat for better maintenance of body temperature. Unknowingly, they may have been creating the ability to glide and then fly.

Another fossil, *Hesperornis*, estimated at 90 million years old, was much larger than Loons of today. It was five to six feet long and well-adapted for diving. It was totally flightless and had solid bones, unlike the hollow, lightweight bones typical in birds capable of flight. Loons also possess solid bones to attain a specific gravity near that of water. Bones filled with air spaces would provide too much buoyancy for avid divers such as Loons. Although the extinct *Hesperornis* and today's Loons adapted toward similar niches, they also traveled down different paths of evolution.

SONG

The Common Loon is probably most famous for its primitive sounding calls. Once heard, they are not easily forgotten. Those people who inhabit the north country feel these sounds represent the symbol of wilderness, the symbol of the ages. In its repetiore the Common Loon has four distinct calls. The most commonly heard is the "wail", a loud and beautiful call that may be heard for miles. It is often given at night to locate other Loons or possibly as a signal indicating desire to exchange places on the nest. It is interesting that during this call the bill is nearly closed.

The "tremolo", a rapid laughing call, is usually given in alarm but may be used for many purposes. It is the only call given in flight and may serve in communication with other migrating Common Loons.

Another complex song called a "yodel" is given by males, only for territorial purposes. It is a warning to other Loons to stay away, lest they be driven away. The "yodel" appears to vary in each male Loon, thus enabling biologists to identify birds without difficult capturing and banding.

Finally, there is the "hoot". Usually uttered very softly between family members, it may be for intimate communication between mated pairs or as various signals to the chicks.

Often, during the vocal nights of summer, Common Loons combine these calls into a beautiful music. To lie awake in north country listening to these beautiful creatures is an experience that stirs the soul.

Unfortunately, the Loon is silent on its winter range; appearing only as a large, nondescript bird of the coasts. If more people could hear its call, they might be reminded of their ties with our environment. It is important that we do not live merely *on* the land, but with it. Too often man feels that with his brief wisdom he can improve what Nature has taken millions of years to create.

DESCRIPTION

The Common Loon is the only one of the four species to nest in the lower 48 states. Its breeding range reaches the upper north-central and northeastern states, although the majority of nests are in Canada.

Wintering areas occur along the Pacific, Atlantic, and Gulf coasts, with some individuals wintering on large bodies of water near the coasts. Common Loons do not have specific migratory routes and often stop and rest on lakes throughout much of the interior United States.

Most Common Loons weigh between seven and thirteen pounds with males generally larger than females. Their body length ranges from 28 to 35 inches and they possess a wingspan over 50 inches across. Though relatively small for such a heavy bird, the wings create a loud sound in flight. The head is broad and equipped with a long, powerful bill. The Common Loon's eyes are red, which against the very dark green head of breeding plummage, gives a haunting appearance. The white barring on the neck of these breeding birds is brilliant. The black back has many white spots of varying size. Such a contrasting pattern of black and white camouflages the Common Loon when reflected on the sunlit water. The lower submerged portions of the Loon are whitish, which probably aids in disguising the Loon's presence from prey species below. The plummage of both sexes is similar.

In August, the adults replace the spectacular breeding plummage by molting into a drab winter coloring that resembles juvenile birds. Basically, these Loons are dark above and light below. Even the bill becomes paler in color. The beauty that has graced the northern lakes must pass, as does all life that summer brings, only to create an excitement for its return.

The Common Loon may live between fifteen and thirty years. The average life span is probably much less, in large part due

to man's activities. Finally, before the remaining three species are described, the prospective Loon watcher should remember that the Common Loon is the only species with a dark head and bill in summer. These two characteristics will make correct identification easier if other species are present during spring migration.

The Arctic Loon is smaller, with a body length from 23 to 29 inches and a wing span under 50 inches. It weighs approximately five pounds and has a beautiful silver-gray head with long white stripes on a black throat. Its black back has white spots larger and fewer in number than the Common Loon. Its call is not as elaborate – sometimes resembling a whistle. In winter, the Arctic Loon is drab colored much like the Common Loons. Arctic Loons breed farther north in central and northwest Canada and Alaska. They winter along the Pacific coast with rare sitings on the Atlantic coast.

The Red-throated Loon is the smallest of the four species, weighing approximately four pounds. On the breeding grounds it has a brilliant red throat patch and white stripes on the back of a grayish head and neck. The back is a dark blackish-gray and does not possess the flashy white spots found on the other three species. Its dark bill is not as stout and is noticeably upturned. The song resembles the quacking sounds of ducks but is given in a series. It can occupy smaller bodies of water than the other species because it needs less room for a running take-off. This fact probably contributes to its being the most abundant Loon on the Canadian and Alaskan arctic. The Red-throated Loon winters along both North American coasts but the northern Atlantic coast receives the largest concentrations.

Our last species, the Yellow-billed Loon, is also the largest Loon, averaging between

CONTINUED ON PAGE EIGHTEEN

ten and fourteen pounds. Its plummage is very similar to the Common Loon's but is easily distinguished by its pale yellow to ivory colored bill. Also, the lower portion of the bill is prominently upturned. Its entire breeding range is north of the Arctic circle and it winters primarily along the northern Pacific coast. The call is similar to the Common Loon but is harsher and louder.

All Loons are relatively large birds and are highly adapted for aquatic life, as well they should be. Only a small fraction of their life is spent on land or in flight. They are excellent divers, with legs located extremely far back on their bodies and large, powerful webbed feet. This positioning has evolved primarily for mobility in water, which has made locomotion on land nearly impossible. So remarkable are their aquatic skills that they can control their visible presence by swimming on top of the water, half-submerged, or with only the head above the surface. Their practically solid bones and unique regulation of air enables these varying levels of visibility. Normally, internal air sacs used for cooling, buoyancy, and respiration would prevent such aquatic capabilities. Loons, however, can compress the air from their lungs, plummage, and air sacs, allowing them to easily submerge. This ability has undoubtedly aided their survival and modified their daily activities.

Loons often swim with their head below the surface to sight prey before diving. The average feeding dives generally last under one minute with their longest dives probably under five minutes in length. Common Loons are sneaky and can obtain a breath by barely breaking the surface, giving the appearance of much longer dives.

It is difficult to determine the greatest depth Loons have reached. It is probably safe to estimate that such masterful divers have attained depths of 100 to 150 feet. The majority of dives, however, are much shallower. The inability to see prey in deep water and the need to conserve energy would support this statement. Also, the Loon's eye appears red because it reflects red wavelengths. At depths below 15 feet only the blue portion of visible light is present. The Loon's eye can absorb these wavelengths thereby making vision possible. This is simply one more remarkable trait in the Loon's specialization for aquatic life.

The water environment also creates higher demands on the plummage of Loons. The feathers of most birds need continual maintenance to preserve their quality, appearance and function. The uropygial gland located on the rump secretes a waterproofing substance of fatty acids and wax. The Loon emits this oily substance onto the bill for transfer to the feathers. Preening, as it is called, is especially important in aquatic birds to prevent feathers from becoming matted. Also, during preening a fundamental interlocking mechanism that is characteristic of feather vanes becomes more resistant to deterioration. It furthermore prevents the bill from drying and sloughing. The uropygial gland is so important that a severe malfunction may result in the death of that individual.

MIGRATION

Loons may be highly adapted to an aquatic lifestyle, but flight, the fundamental characteristic of birds, still ensures the survival of their species. Migration is needed to travel from oceanic coasts to nesting areas in regions of North America where competition is reduced. There are also fewer factors that contribute to the death of young on these northern lakes, which adds to their appeal.

Unfortunately, the Loon's heavy body weight makes flight extremely difficult. Most Common Loons need one quarter mile of water for a running take-off. Once in the air constant flapping allows them to remain airborne.

Other factors also increase the risk of travel for Loons during migration. It is impossible for a Loon to take-off from land and many Loons die after landing on wet pavement that looks deceivingly like a body of water. Although these factors may claim some Loons each year, the overall migration has been successful for centuries.

The Common Loon flies very fast, achieving speeds from 60 to 100 miles per hour. This quick flight undoubtedly enables long migrations and reduces the hazard of flying over land. Migration generally occurs during daylight hours with their legs extended behind and their neck somewhat shortened.

Their comfort with water is illustrated even in migration. Flight is only a few feet above the water, but over land the Loon may migrate at altitudes of 1500 feet. They also travel in small numbers, usually spread out to better locate bodies of water for stopovers. Often, when bad weather prevails, migration will cease to eliminate the chance of being forced to the ground and perishing.

The mystery of bird migration has puzzled biologists for many years. In many species, juvenile birds flock with older birds that have traveled the migratory routes. Loons, on the other hand, may travel alone or even in flocks of juveniles in late fall. Other theories infer that birds use celestial or solar orientation. On nights of heavy cloud cover birds may use the earth's magnetism for direction. Although birds do have navigational ability to return year after year to the same nesting area no single method is possible. Probably a combination of these and other cues are used.

ORTHERN LAKES
ARE THE
BREEDING
GROUNDS
OF THE
LOONS

The growing season in the northland where Loons nest is much shorter than that of most latitudes where humans populate the lower 48 states. It is critical that Loons begin nesting activities as soon as their lakes become free of ice to ensure that their young will be developed enough to fly before the ice returns in the fall.

During the month of May Loons arrive on many lakes only one or two days after the ice withdraws. The males usually arrive first and start defining a territory. Their nesting site requirements are simple and logical. A sufficient food supply in clear water is needed to support incubating adults and growing young. The actual nest site should be secluded, such as an island, allowing protection from weather with an easy access into relatively deep water. Also, island nest sites are preferred to eliminate most predation. Finally, areas of shallow water protected from the wind are desirable. The total area may be 400 acres, and most pairs need a minimum of 50 acres.

As the male establishes the territory, yodel calls make his presence known to all possible intruders. Even fish-eating waterfowl such as Mergansers are warded off as competitors. Soon, the female arrives and both birds call back and forth to one another, possibly in relief that migration is over and with anticipation of nesting.

It is curious that although Loons mate for life, they do not migrate or winter together. Their calling may be to strengthen bonds in the first stage of courtship. During these first few days courtship behavior will be a large part of their daily activities. Their displays are ritualized, as in most birds, to eliminate breeding with individuals of other species. Their courtship displays may include dipping and/or jerking the bill into the water, head movements from side to side, and circling. Even a ritualized preening may be a form of courtship. Finally, the female leaves the water and calls softly from land to the male. It is here that copulation must occur, for water cannot support the weight of both birds. Copulation occurs frequently while the specific nest site is being determined.

Common Loons will use the same nest sites year after year. If the site has been disturbed or destroyed the pair may simply abandon nesting activities. In the same sense, the nest site, if still intact, may be used after the area has become increasingly inhabited or visited by man. This adaptation toward cohabitation has become very important to Loons' survival as human activity continues to increase in their breeding range. After their nest site is selected, the territory is more intensely defended. Their antagonistic behavior most often involves calling, but intruding Loons may be driven

CONTINUED ON PAGE TWENTY-NINE

away physically. Such confrontations are rarely fatal. Confrontations with other waterfowl or raccoons are not as passive. These species are competitors or predators which directly threaten the niche inhabited by Loons. Such an intrusion is not accepted in nature.

Both sexes may participate in building the crude nest usually located within two feet of the water's edge. It is composed of small amounts of available ferns, grasses, or weeds. Only a small depression is needed because both parents take turns to constantly incubate the required 28–30 days. Two greenish to brownish eggs with dark spots are laid over a three day period. They are oval, and approximately two inches by three inches, and must be kept at temperatures near 95 degrees Fahrenheit. Shifts generally last a couple of hours while the resting bird feeds but may range from only 30 minutes to six hours. Incubation is very demanding as black flies are a continual annoyance and alertness is constantly needed.

Predators such as mink, weasel, skunks,

raccoon, otters, crows, and gulls are always on the lookout for an easy meal. The adult birds maintain a low profile on the nest to avoid detection but predation often occurs. The Loons may be disturbed and leave the nest, leaving the eggs unprotected. If one of these predators finds a nest unattended, it is possible for the Loons to renest, although the success rate is low. This factor probably explains why some Loons on the nest can be approached by man. Usually, upon approach, the brooding bird will slip into the water and try to distract the intruder away from the nest. If it is a predator which is not fooled, renesting may occur as late as mid-June – but generally not later.

When man approaches and with the knowledge that Loons could be nesting, he should heed the warning and leave. Unbrooded eggs left for very long may chill and will not hatch. It is unfortunate and often unknowingly that people will see and pursue Loons simply out of curiosity and as spectators of their beauty. In some areas the Memorial

CONTINUED ON PAGE THIRTY-TWO

Day and Fourth of July weekends attract large numbers of people and can critically affect nesting success. Nevertheless, with all these factors, many Loons will hatch a pair of chicks beginning in late June.

Loon chicks usually hatch a day or two apart and are covered with black down. They are precocial like many ground nesters and can leave the nest within a few hours after hatching. Loons hatching two chicks are lucky and have passed the most crucial stage in reproduction. A large majority of chicks that hatch will survive but many precautions still remain to successfully endure the growing and learning months of summer.

Loon chicks are very buoyant and tire easily. They spend much of their time riding on the backs of their parents between the wings. The adults assist boarding by submerging partially for the chicks. It is not only a place to rest and dry, but it provides protection from snapping turtles, birds, and large fish. Soon, the adults

begin bringing small prey species such as small fish, snails, frogs, crayfish, and small insects for the young to swallow whole.

By three weeks of age, the chicks are half the size of adults and have molted into a yellow plummage. The adults now stun their prey by slapping it on the water. It is then released for the young Loons to capture and eat. As the chicks grow in size their diving skills increase rapidly, and they are led into deeper water. Here adults begin releasing prey only slightly injured to improve the diving and feeding skills of their chicks.

As the family group ventures away from the nesting area toward deeper water, the chance for interaction with other species is increased. It is therefore important that the Loons have a method to avoid potential danger. For example, if a man approached a family group of Loons the young would be instructed to

CONTINUED ON PAGE THIRTY-SIX

hide near the shoreline if possible. Warning calls would be given, and adults may become frantic if distraction displays fail. As a last resort, an adult may run upright across the water with its neck curled back in what is called the "penguin dance". It is spectacular, but man should immediately leave if this behavior should occur.

As summer passes quickly, the young Loons acquire a drab plummage while adults begin molting their magnificent breeding dress for a similar drab attire. During this time both adults and juveniles are flightless. Feeding dominates their activities in order to gain size and build fat reserves to make possible the long flight to the wintering grounds. Most species of fish, including minnows, bluegill, trout, pike, and bass, are consumed, along with various invertebrates already mentioned. The availability of prey tends to be the determining factor that regulates their diet. After a summer capturing prey, the young Loons perfect diving and "sinking" abilities thereby enabling a gradual decrease of their dependence on the parents. Only one skill is left to be taught – the art of flight.

In late August and early September the parents drill the young with races across the top of the water. The chase continues daily up and down the lake until the juveniles attain flight at approximately eleven weeks of age. It must be a glorious and frightening experience the first time flight is achieved. The endless aquatic environment that has dominated their life thus far becomes a defined, reflective surface. Their new experiences at flying are brief at first, but slowly the flight muscles strengthen and they are capable of migrating to distant waters. Yet, this lake has been their home and they are reluctant to leave.

The parents, having completed respon-sibilities toward their young and the species, simply depart one day. The reluctant juveniles are left alone and do not depart until as late as early November. There is always the possibility that the ice will come and prevent take-off. Perhaps this is one of the many tests for juvenile birds. Nature ensures that each species of wild things will evolve toward perfection.

The fall migration is casual and Loons often

stop, rest, and replenish their energy reserves. This generally results in small congregations of Loons (less than 100) forming on traditional lakes of staging along the migratory routes. The bond that has held adult Loons together is removed and they become separated. The late migrating juveniles must rely on instinct for there are no adults to show them the way. It is amazing that such a long trip over changing landscapes can be made without guidance from others. Yet the young Loons travel onward, trusting the genes passed to them from generations past. It will be three years before they are sexually mature and return to the north country where they were raised. The ocean will be their new home.

The Atlantic Ocean provides an aquatic environment for which Common Loons are specialized. The largest concentrations of wintering Loons are off the coasts of the middle New England states. Here, life is much different from the freshwater continental lakes and requires some stressful adjustments.

First, Loons must adapt to the salt concentration of the sea water. This is done by secreting excess salt accumulated in the blood through a nasal salt gland that is found in most oceanic birds. Their food sources now include flounder, cod, herring, sea trout, mackerel, and crabs along with many other species. Feeding usually corresponds with the prey that tides bring with them twice a day. Each Loon's feeding territory is generally separated by 150 yards or more.

Preening also becomes a major occupation to combat the harsh affects of salt water. At night, Loons may raft together where mutual prevention may possibly be used to avoid being washed up on shore. The ocean is harsh, but it provides a supporting environment for these drab looking birds to live.

Later, when the sexually mature Loons leave during the summer months for the northern breeding grounds, the juvenile birds benefit from less competition. This factor, along with practically no predators, has made oceanic life a suitable habitat for juvenile Loons to mature. Regrettably, though, Loons must also cope with the activities of man that upset the fragile natural balance of their wild environment.

In recent years, man has been a hazard to Loons and most other species of wildlife. Large oil spills have occurred, coating the feathers of birds. Oil is often ingested and most birds cannot be saved even if still alive after washing ashore. Commercial fishing has also taken its toll as Loons are attracted to the concentrations of fish created by this activity. Upon pursuit of easy prey, Loons often become entangled in the nets and drown. The multitude of chemicals we have unnaturally placed into our environment may also have affected the overall state of health of the Loon population. Hydro-electric power dams now allow man to regulate lake levels, often at the Loons' expense. Frequently, the water levels during nesting have been raised, inundating the nest. At other times levels have been allowed to drop, leaving the nest far from water.

The appeal of the north country as a summer home for people has also had its dramatic effects. Besides typical harassment, the shorelines of northern lakes have become developed, destroying valuable habitat of the Common Loon. Habitat loss has determined the fate of many species even if other factors are ideal. The increase in people inhabiting the breeding grounds also brings more garbage. This in turn has increased the populations of gulls and raccoons which prey heavily on Loon eggs and chicks.

Probably the most devastating effect produced by man is the onslaught of acid rain.

The combustion of fossil fuels in automobiles and more specifically coal-burning industries have produced this tragic problem. Acid anhydrides (gases that combine with water to form acids) such as carbon dioxide, sulfur dioxide, and various nitrogen oxides are precipitated into many of our northern lakes, lowering their ph to sterile levels. The acid rain also releases mercury from the soil and rocks that may enter the food chain. Mercury concentrations then slowly increase in Loons and other wildlife. The concentrated mercury, when combined with other factors, may then result in death of Common Loons. The vast number of northern lakes being affected by acid rain is growing at an alarming rate. This is a problem that must be corrected for the sake of Loons and of Man.

The mortality by natural factors of Common Loons include disease-causing organisms, parasites, migration hazards, and stress. One such factor has increased in the last twenty years. Botulism, an anaerobic bacteria, has caused significant die-offs of waterfowl and Loons. It is contracted by Loons through contaminated baitfish and has been a rare but lethal disease. The exact location botulism will occur is difficult to determine and no prevention is known.

The future of the Common Loon is not certain. It appears to be adapting to areas of nesting where human inhabitation is relatively

CONTINUED ON PAGE FORTY-FOUR

high. Loons nesting on these lakes do not flush as readily as those on low-populated lakes. The use of artificial nesting platforms is also a positive sign. Most importantly the public is being educated about the values of our native wildlife. In particular, a romance between people and the Common Loon is growing, and many organizations have been formed to aid in their survival. Finally, the dedication of many people, both professional and amateur, has greatly enhanced knowledge of the Common Loon. They have been captivated and may view this creature as a symbol representing all things wild. Swimming quietly across a mirror-still lake, signifies peace. Suddenly, the Loon calls, as a cry of the wild, with all focus on it and it alone. It may be a cry for man to live in harmony with nature for the very survival of the world. The world is like any other organism. It fights for life, but as the injuries and disease increase, it must submit. Henry David Thoreau tried to convey this important message when he wrote;

"In wilderness is the preservation of the world".

The complex interrelationships in nature by many species ensures stability. It can be compared to a spider's web; the more strands intercrossing, the stronger the web. If many of the strands are eliminated, the web becomes weak and loses its function.

As stewards of this land, we must protect our environment and our Loons, for they are an integral part of our future. The destiny of man is previewed by the plight of wilderness and wildlife. Man came and he conquered. Today, the ultimate challenge awaits him – the challenge to conquer his mistakes and renew his environment.

SELECTED REFERENCES

Dunning, Joan, *The Loon – Voice of the Wilderness*, Yankee Books, Dublin, NH 1985
Hollatz, Tom, *The Loon Book*, North Star Press, St. Cloud, Mn 1984
Klein, Tom, *Loon Magic*, Paper Birch Press Inc., Ashland, WI 1985
Peterson, Roger T., *A Field Guide to the Birds*, Houghton Mifflin Co., Boston 1980
Pettingill, Jr., Olin S., *Ornithology in Laboratory and Field*, Burgess Publishing Co., 1970